When Moving on Hurts

A Memoir

By Kyra King

For more information, email info@prosperlogisticsllc.com.

DEDICATION

I dedicate this book to every woman who feels the pain of moving on, but knows it is time to leave her toxic relationship—those who dared to wipe their tears and overcame trials and tribulations. For the risk takers that choose to bet on themselves and keep tunnel vision to become successful and truly happy with their life journey, I salute you.

To my family, I know you only want the best for me. There were many situations in which you had no idea what I went through. However, I made it with God's protection, a praying mother, father, and a great support system.

To my children, I love you more than anything in this world. My children kept me here. Their love is the greatest love I have ever experienced. I love you more than any other. When you are older and move throughout life, keep God first ALWAYS, never ignore red flags with any situation, and always know your worth. I love you both, your mommy.

TABLE OF CONTENTS

Introduction

I want to leave, but I can't. I love him so much and I want to make this work, but I know this relationship isn't right. I don't want to be alone and have to start all over again. How am I supposed to pick up the pieces and move forward?

If you have ever experienced an abusive relationship, then most likely you experienced feelings of worthlessness, self-doubt, insecurity, and confusion. Many women are involved in abusive relationships but are scared to speak up. There are women who want to leave but fear they can't live without their abuser. Being in a narcissistic abusive relationship can have severe consequences on a person's physical, mental, and emotional well-being. Breaking the chains of abuse and reclaiming your power is a difficult, but empowering journey.

It can be expected for women to have it all together and wear the title of "Super Woman." As a result, we often wear a mask to hide all the pain and tend to suppress our true feelings and handle our business by any means necessary. According to a study by the National Domestic Violence

Hotline, approximately 1 in 6 women have experienced narcissistic abuse, which is a form of emotional abuse characterized by manipulation, control, and power imbalances. Additionally, another survey found that women accounted for 85% of victims of narcissistic abuse.

The problem is that many women stay in abusive relationships because they feel financially dependent on their abuser, while others may feel emotionally invested in the relationship or may fear retaliation if they leave. Some individuals may lack support systems or may not be aware of resources available to them.

The solution is to educate yourself about healthy relationships and to be aware of red flags that may indicate a potentially unhealthy or abusive relationship. Healing from narcissistic abuse is a journey and it may take time. Be patient with yourself and seek support when needed. It is important to prioritize your own well-being and make sure that your needs and boundaries are respected in any future relationships. This will allow you to gain insight and strength, to move forward in a positive direction.

Purpose

I am Kyra King; I am the author of *When Moving on Hurts.* I wrote this book to share my story on how I overcame and survived an abusive relationship and to also help women suffering in abusive relationships go from VICTIM to VICTOR, by being able to identify, tackle, and conquer narcissistic abuse.

The purpose of this book is to remind women they are worthy of true love and they do not have to be a victim to any form of abuse. Don't ever ignore your intuition, no matter how good things may feel. Your intuition is God's protection, warning you of what you can't see. Keep God first and to never ignore red flags.

Life is a journey, enjoy your journey and don’t ever compare it to someone else's. Dig deep to love and learn your inner self to reach your higher being and your true calling on why God placed you here. Grab your wine and enjoy reading how I went from Victim to Victorious.

CHAPTER 1

WHERE IT BEGAN

CHAPTER 1

WHERE IT BEGAN

I am Kyra King. I was born in Joliet, Illinois, and raised in south Atlanta in Clayton County. I am the youngest of three children. My mom has been the greatest influence in my life and raised me to be the woman I am today. She became a single mom when my parents divorced when I was five. Before the divorce, I remember being both a daddy's and a mommy's girl. However, once my parents split, I stayed and spent more time with my mom and her family.

I spent most of my childhood at basketball practice, traveling to basketball games, and vacationing with my family. I had an amazing childhood and never lacked anything. I wasn't the kid that grew up in the rough areas of town or didn't have food every night on the table to eat. I grew up with what they call a "silver spoon" in my mouth. Although I did not struggle physically, I suffered mentally. While growing up, I missed my dad being in the home. For most of my childhood, it seemed like I was the only one whose father didn't live at home. All of my friends had active fathers who supported them with school activities and sports. Their dads would take them to practice and attend all their games. My dad came to some of my games but not many.

Remarried

Whenever I visited my dad, I had a great time. On one of my weekend visits, I discovered he had remarried, and I wasn't invited to the wedding. My dad's new wife showed me pictures after they returned home. It was hurtful to know I was not included in the wedding because my dad and I were extremely close. Everything changed as soon as he remarried; the fun and enjoyment ended. I went from being excited to no longer looking forward to seeing him. It hurt to know he had moved on to another wife and stepdaughter.

Although I got along with my dad's new wife, I knew she wasn't genuine and wanted me out of the equation. She always made it known that my dad now has another little girl. When his stepdaughter began calling him "daddy," I can say that this is when I first started gaining resentment about my parents' divorce. I resented my dad because he was an active father in their household to a kid that was not his, but not an involved father to me when he and I shared the same blood. I could not understand how he went from being my favorite person to a man I looked at as a babysitter after a while.

To make things worse, my dad's stepdaughter and I shared the same birthday. Every year he faced the difficult decision of whose birthday celebration he would attend. There were many times he could make it to my birthday celebration, and there were times when he missed it because he celebrated with his stepdaughter. This was when our relationship began to fall apart.

Years later, my father was incarcerated. From there, I always searched for a father figure. My stepmom took me twice to visit him. I went years without seeing my dad because my stepmom did not make an effort to ensure I saw my father. She was the only adult on the list to bring me. I would reach out to see my little brother and keep relations, all failures. I would only visit my dad and see my little brother when my grandmother was in town.

As I grew older, I had more questions. My mom told me what type of person my stepmom was and how she did not respect my parents' marriage. This also made me resent my dad more. As a result, I did not want to visit them, and I was ok with a phone call instead.

Bittersweet

The relationship between my dad and I is bittersweet. I still remember when he would take me to all the Atlanta Hawks games in our matching suits and smile. However, I also think about when he left, and all the days I needed him more. I learned to forgive him and took accountability for not forgiving him sooner to rebuild our relationship. Today, my dad and I are best friends. He's my rider and business guru. He owns a business and helps me whenever I call on him. I spent most of my twenties voicing how I felt and telling him how I felt about many things that affected me growing up.

While in college, he would drive four hours to my school to spend time with me on the weekends. Once I graduated from college, he took me on my first trip to Washington, DC. It was the ideal location for me to ensure a successful career. My dad often would listen to me go off on him and text or call me the following day, showing that he is still my father who loves me through my breakdowns. I know he is proud of me because I also get my hustle mentality from him. I admire that I can talk to him about anything. Every day, we work on fixing our relationship and making up for lost time. Besides that, my childhood was pretty awesome. I experienced a lot of fun and happy times when I wasn't dwelling on things out of my control. It wasn't until adulthood that I experienced life lessons and faced adversity.

Everybody's Superwoman

I idolized my mom my whole childhood and wanted to grow up to be just like her; she was such a boss. She held top company positions throughout my life, including Regional Director at a beauty school. She won many awards for her leadership, and everyone loved her. My mom is a pretty lady, so the beauty industry came easy for her. She ran multiple schools in and out of Georgia. Every year, we took trips with her company to attend the Bronner Brothers' hair show. The Bronner Brothers' hair show is the world's largest professional trade show dedicated to multicultural beauty. My sisters and I looked forward to that event. It was amazing to see all of the creative hair stylists.

My mom was everybody's superwoman. There wasn't anything she couldn't do. On top of that, this woman spoiled us beyond words. Even to this day, my sisters and I lack nothing; our kids lack nothing. Every Christmas, she provides us with an entire box of surprises. She was not the parent that let go once we turned 18. If anything, she grew closer to our children and to us.

We lived in a big ranch-style house with a huge backyard and a perfect golf course view. The view of the golf course was beautiful, but my mom always had to replace our kitchen window every other month because of flying golf balls. My mom was passionate about interior design and made our home a masterpiece. The floors in our house were marble, the colors of the walls and furniture were perfectly coordinated, and each bedroom had its own unique design.

My favorite part was my basketball court located in the driveway in front of the house. Many nights I would be outside playing with the boys, talking smack that I could beat them, and I did. Those were the times I enjoyed and grew a passion for basketball, my first love. Basketball became my first coping mechanism to deal with what I was facing mentally from my parents' separation.

I watched my mom get up in the morning, fix breakfast, and drive my middle sister and I to a private school on the other side of town. From there, she took my sister home and then took me to basketball practice, which was also on the other side of town. To this day, I still do not see how she managed so many tasks for one person. My older sister attended the local high school in the neighborhood. She was smarter than my sister and I and did not need extra help or discipline, LOL. She skipped a grade. She stayed to herself and enjoyed reading books. Her friends came over from time to time, which was fun, but she ran her own show and stayed out of the way. My mom did not have many problems from her. My middle sister and I were close in age, so many of our peers knew we were siblings. We fought a lot growing up but were always there for one another. If someone wanted to fight me, then she fought them. If somebody wanted to fight her, then I fought them. That is how our relationship was growing up. We could not stand each other, but literally would beat anybody up about each other. Today, I am close to both sisters and love them both dearly.

Prayer During Adversity

Dear God,

In the face of adversity, I come to You seeking strength and guidance. Help me to trust in Your plans, even when it feels difficult and uncertain. Give me the courage to face my challenges with grace and resilience, knowing that You are always with me, even in the darkest times.

I pray for strength, perseverance, and faith as I navigate the trials of this life. May Your light shine upon me always, and may I find peace in Your presence.

In Jesus' Name, Amen.

Chapter 2

Love Bombing

CHAPTER 2

LOVE BOMBING

The Love Bombing Stage is the first stage of abuse. During this stage, the abuser showers you with romantic dates, gifts, love, and kisses. They will rush into the "I love you" phase. They will make you feel like you are the best in the world and living in a fairytale. This stage will feel too good to be true. The abuser will also want all your time during this period and will want to isolate you from family and friends. Lastly, during this stage you are blinded to what you think is love and will do anything to keep the feeling going.

The Stare Down

It was a late night in April of 2019, and I had gotten out of boot camp with Queen Warrior B (Instagram page: @Warrior_queenb). Her workouts are intense and rewarding. She instilled so much confidence in her clients. I was exhausted and hungry. No food spots were open that I wanted to eat from, so I settled for a smoothie at LA Fitness.

While waiting on my smoothie, I zoned out watching others working out, sweat dripping from their bodies, and music playing. I could hear the sneakers from the basketball court in the back of the building of people getting more work in. Then, a fine dark skin man, wearing jeans, with his hat turned backwards was leaving the gym and staring at me. Our eyes locked and I couldn't stop staring back. I thought he was so fine. Neither of us spoke, and we both stared. My Super Green Giant smoothie was finished, so I left the gym. There was a black Jeep parked out front. I hoped it was him and behold it was. There was a voice yelling towards me asking if I had a boyfriend. I responded, "No," and he asked for my number with a huge smile on his face. We exchanged numbers. I was on the phone with my mom walking to my car. When she heard him, she immediately said, *"Kyra keep walking and get to your car safely please."* I should have listened that night, I should have kept walking.

We didn't text that night and I was fine with that. I had to go to work in the morning and needed a good night's rest. The connection I felt with the stare down was enough for the night.

Strictly Entertainment

The next morning, I got up and went to work. I did my normal routine of waking up and getting my son and I ready for the day. My son's daycare was close to my office. We would sometimes stop for McDonald's oatmeal, especially if we were running late and I did not have time to fix breakfast. My life was simple and good, I had no complaints. I was twenty-five years old and promoted to Detective at the local Police Department. I had my own everything. I was a boss mom. I never put too much time and attention into dating. This was the first time I seriously considered dating after it was only my son and I.

All morning I thought about the man I met last night at the gym. It was something that made me want to give him my number. Around noon, I got a text, and it was him. He asked me how I was doing. We then got into a personal conversation about how many children we each had. I responded with one, a two-year-old son, named Grayson. He told me he had four children. At that time, I knew I was not going to take him seriously. No offense, but that was too many kids for me for one man. It was crazy because his next text was, "*Don't judge me.*" Hahaha. He must have read my mind because I sure was. He told me he had three kids with one girl, who he had been with for 10 years. He also had a daughter with another girl. I decided to still text him for entertainment, strictly entertainment. He then invited me to lunch at a well-known pizza joint.

The lunch date went well. While sitting at the table, I didn't notice with the first stare down how light his eyes were. They were gorgeous and reminded me of my grandfather's. His eyes were burnt orange with a touch of brown. Guys with colored eyes are my weakness. I reminded myself that he has four kids and two baby mamas, and this is not what I wanted. The pizza came and I wanted to stuff my face, but instead I kept it cute.

A few days later, he invited me out again. We decided to meet at a restaurant in Atlanta. Even though the restaurant was a little ghetto, it had great music and good drinks. Towards the end of the night, the DJ played slow, seductive, and romantic music. The mood was right, the drinks kicked in, and he slid in for a kiss. What I thought was only entertainment turned out to be something I didn't expect. I really liked this dude with the kids. Over the next few weeks, we continued to text. Texting evolved into more fun dates, good food, and positive vibes. We were like two teenage kids living in the moment. It got to the point that I would call out of work to hang out with him. It progressed from the dates to me coming to his house.

Love at First Sight

The first time I visited him at his home in South Georgia, I was impressed. It was a nice ranch home built entirely of brick. The lawn was huge and the houses in the wealthy neighborhood screamed, "paid." Y'all get it, it was upscale and fancy. However, something in my head alerted me to a red flag when he told me to park in the second driveway. This was not the main one that led to the house. He previously told me he owned his home, so I didn't understand why it mattered where I parked or what entrance I came in. I ignored it and continued to park. Once I parked, he came out and greeted me. We entered from the back of the house into the basement. Another red flag! I asked him why we had to enter through the basement. He responded, his mom and two sisters have the upstairs, and he lets them stay with him. Another red flag. His sisters were older than me and his mom was a pastor and prophet. I felt more at ease knowing he came from a God-fearing family, because his mom preached the Word, or so I thought.

He cooked for me every time I came over. We had everything from T-bone steaks, seafood dishes, soul food, fish and grits, oxtails, lamb chops, and BBQ on the grill. I have never met a man in my life besides my uncle and brother-in-law, who knew how to cook for real. Everything Nathan cooked made me want to "slap my mama."

We watched movies and discovered our music taste was the exact same. This has never happened to me. We both loved R&B music from back in the day. It was always music that connected us. This was everything, not only the type of music, but also the ad libs, and the smooth beat.

I do not know how it happened, but at this point I am in love! Crazy, right? Yeah, I know. He told me that he loved me first and not that I felt obligated, but I felt as though I loved him as well. The love between us was mutual and he became my best friend. There was nothing I wanted to do that he did not make happen. Our conversations and connection were unforced. I loved being around him. There was not one second that we wanted to be a part.

My mom spotted the red flags early on and I ignored every word. I was having fun and finally enjoying someone I loved. She knew I was spending too much time with him too soon. I didn't look at it that way at the time. I looked at it as if I was having fun, my bills were paid, and life was great. Why not date and see where it goes? I felt at this moment, love at first sight existed.

South Florida

In May 2019, we traveled to South Florida for the weekend. It was hot and the temperature was calling for it. All I wanted to do was eat more delicious food, drink, lay on the beach, and escape my reality. Once we arrived, he rented the best resort on the beach. We were right on the ocean; the view was amazing. I could see the clear blue water. The beautiful sun and the palm trees were sensational. All he kept saying to me was whatever you want to do, let's do it. I felt like a spoiled kid. We went shopping, rode jet skis, rented a motorcycle (I looked fine on the back), and ate good food.

We returned home. I practically moved in with him due to the amount of time I spent there. I met all four of his children, fell in love with them and accepted the reality of the four. However, in my family, it's not looked upon as favorable to marry or date a man with a certain number of children. My family's standards are pretty high. If you bring somebody home for Thanksgiving or Christmas, they better be of high caliber, or you will see it on a cousin's, uncle's, or aunt's face. You will not get judged, but you will get talked about. I knew my mom would think I was crazy to be in love with a man with so many kids and more than one baby mama. She would probably think I had lost my mind. I knew I would have to hear her spill. Looking back, she always wanted the best for me, but of course I was stuck in my head. Crazy because I did not care. I loved him and I was going to continue to love him. It seemed like, as soon as I expressed my love to him, the arguments started to pick up. We argued about everything.

PRAYER FOR GUIDANCE

Dear God,

I come to You, seeking guidance and direction. I know You have a plan for my life, and I trust that Your plan is perfect and good. Please give me clarity and understanding as I seek your direction. Please reveal the path you want me to take and give me the courage to follow it, even if it is difficult.

Thank you for Your love and grace and for always being there for me. I trust in Your unfailing love and know You will guide me in the right direction.

In Jesus' name, Amen.

Chapter 3

Gaslighting

CHAPTER 3

GASLIGHTING

During the Gaslighting Stage, the Narcissist begins to devalue the victim by criticizing them, belittling them, and making them feel unworthy. They use gaslighting and other manipulative tactics to make the victim doubt their own perceptions and feelings. This can make it difficult for the victim to trust their judgment and make decisions independently, leading to confusion and self-doubt. Victims become more reliant on the abuser for validation and guidance.

Crazy Connection

We continued to travel. We took a trip to Gatlinburg, Tennessee. It was different from the normal vacation destinations that we had previously visited, but we had so much fun. Our trip included horseback riding, ziplining, go-karting, and staying in a cabin. The cabin had a pool table, and we played a few games. We were both athletes in high school, so the competitiveness was always there. We stayed competing and talking junk to one another. At times, I loved it, but other times I hated it because I was still a bit sensitive and emotional, especially if I lost. This man even had us playing hide and seek in the dark. We were being spontaneous, knowing we were so scared in the middle of nowhere in our cabin. It was a crazy connection; we were inseparable. There were red flags throughout the situation, but I ignored them because I liked him and enjoyed the time spent with him. My mind went back and forth, wondering if this was love at first sight or if this man was strange, moving too fast and showing so much love.

We had conversations about life and what we saw in the future. However, one thing that we disagreed on was starting a family. For me, it was soon to be thinking about having a baby with him. I could not understand why he was so desperate to have a child with me; he already had four. Nathan's youngest child was only one. I was afraid of birth control because of the horror stories I heard regarding the side effects. I shared these feelings with Nathan and trusted that he would be careful once we stopped using protection, but he ignored me. The first pregnancy happened, and I was so close to keeping it; however, that pregnancy was terminated.

A Female's Voice

Days later, my son and I were at his house. He was making dinner and decided to jump in the shower. My son was on Nathan's tablet. A number continued to call; I thought maybe it was one of his children, he Facetimed them often, but the number was not saved. I began to have doubts. I wrote the number down and saved it in my phone to call later to see who would answer. I then called the number to see who would answer. It was a female's voice. I went to the text messages and saw that her name was Raegan. If you have an iPhone, you know when the iCloud is connected, the messages will appear on the tablet. Once Nathan was out of the shower. I sat quietly for about 10 minutes trying hard not to assume. I could not help, but to ask. Here's how it went...

"Nathan, who is Raegan?" He immediately got offensive and responded, *"Why are you going through my phone."* He was so stressed; he did not even realize I did not go through his phone. His phone was in the bathroom with him the whole time because he usually liked to play music from his phone when showering. His response was enough for me. Next, he had a look on his face, and I knew it was not good, but I was confused because I was with him day and night; how could he have time to cheat? He looked at me and stated, *"I have something I have to tell you."* My stomach immediately weakened. I knew it had to do with the red flags I ignored. I began to cry and yell at him.

I knew he was going to say he had a baby on the way, he had more kids, he had a family, or something traumatic. There it was, I blurted it out, *"Look, do you have a baby on the way? Did you cheat on me or something?"* Nathan got quiet. At that moment, I went crazy! I mean cuckoo for Coco Puffs. My son was only two years old, and he was so lost. I grabbed him, got our things, and left. I sped out the driveway so fast, thinking, I know I just did not get cheated on, let alone played by what I thought was a fairytale connection. I knew good things didn't last forever; I was pissed. I had to get us away from him and the situation before I spazzed even more. I had to be mindful that I was still a cop. I didn't think jail would be a good idea, and I didn't need to be in anybody's headlines.

Numb Emotions

During the ride home, I was confused about how I was always with him, and he had time to do anything. I wanted to know more, but I could not turn around after I trashed his home. I still had the number, so I called. Again, a female answered. I advised who I was and why I was calling. She responded, *"I am Raegan, Nathan's youngest child's mother, and I am CURRENTLY seven months pregnant with his child; I am due in September."* I almost crashed at this moment. Wait, what?! His youngest daughter, her mother's name is not Raegan; it is Alana. She then responds, *"No, that is a different one, I am the last one, and my name is Raegan."* She further mentions, *"Nathan has six children with this child making baby number seven."* My emotions at this point were numb. I could not believe what she had just told me. I was upset, sad, angry, and lost for words, hoping it was all a dream.

At this moment, I was devastated. How could a person I loved so much and trusted make a fool out of me and lie to me about his children? I was so hurt and broken. I could not believe it. I did not want to believe it. I am home at this point. Of course, he is texting and calling me and her. I responded by text and let him know I knew everything, not just the half-truth he tried to present to me. How could you hide three additional children? I wondered, *"Why did he not care about them?" "Why didn't he spend time with them?"* We had been dating for some time, and I had never heard of or seen these additional children.

Raegan began to tell me; she was also in love with Nathan. He lied and told her he only had three children with one girl he had been with for years. Raegan was devastated. I could hear the hurt in her voice. She was ready to spill all the tea and baby she did. She went on to state that Nathan had messed up her credit, his family was weird, and she knew something was off about him when she had to enter from the side of the house that led to the basement, the same as I did. Nathan advised that he bought the home and let his mother and sisters stay on the upper level. I thought that was odd too, but it was thoughtful, and maybe the man loves taking care of the women in his life, as he was taking care of me.

Depressed and Alone

Raegan and I talked a few days later, and she continued telling me Nathan was a liar. After their first baby was born, he left her in the hospital, depressed and alone. He switched up on her like he never loved her. Raegan suffered from postpartum depression badly. I listened and took notes each time she called, but I still felt empty. I prayed to God for clarity but was still doing what I wanted to do. I was contradicting my own morals and was blind to it.

Nathan wanted to talk after I found out about his truth. I wanted answers, so I met him at the Walmart, down the street from his home. I told him everything Raegan told me. Nathan had a way of finessing his way back in. He cried and apologized for lying about his kids. He said I would have ran from him if he told me about his seven kids at the beginning.

He was right, I would have sprinted away faster than I could blink. I was so upset that he lied and did not give me a choice if I wanted to deal with it or not. I was already deeply in love and depended on his love to function. Instead of walking away and never looking back, I decided to stick beside him.

After finishing our conversation, Raegan called and texted me numerous times about how terrible of a person Nathan was, sending me screenshots that she was in Urgent Care due to having an allergic reaction, and he was ignoring her calls and text messages. She then had the nurse call him, which he also ignored. However, I see her call him and text him asking him to cook for her. She wanted a steak. Was she warning me or trying to move me out the way? My mind was in circles, but I knew the seven kids were valid, and I was still upset and confused.

Tables Continue to Turn

Our relationship did not get any better. Nathan became controlling and abusive. He would get mad if he felt I made eye contact with a guy. If a guy made eye contact with me for too long, he would take it out on me. One night, we went out with a group of our friends. Nathan was on the other side of the club and noticed a guy standing too close to me. The next thing I knew, he rushed to where I was standing, mushed me in front of my friends, and then pushed the man standing next to me, causing him to fall on the floor. Of course, everyone was looking crazy, and security escorted us out. Having stayed with him after the lies, I couldn't understand how he could be so controlling.

Nathan made it clear that I could not have any male friends. Even my best friend from second grade had to be cut off, and my son's Godfather, who was always there for me during college. At this moment, I am at my lowest, not knowing my worth and feeling stuck. I knew to pray but didn't because I was not in a Godly situation. At this moment, I felt embarrassed to go to God because I knew better.

Several weeks passed, and we decided to go to New York to get away and work on being friends. On the day of the flight, he met me at the airport late, which caused us to miss our flight. I was going to get on the plane and fly solo to clear my head. It wasn't my fault he missed the flight, but I allowed them to close the doors and waited for him. When I met him, we looked at each other and laughed. We sat for about 10 minutes until Nathan said, *"Forget it, let's just drive to New Orleans,"* I was with it. We drove to New Orleans, booked our hotel on the spot, and were out. We had the best time in New Orleans. We danced, danced, danced! There was this one spot we went to where we stole the dance floor. Everyone got their phones out and started recording us. We even met another couple while there and partied with them. We went from bar to bar and got wasted! The conversation would come up, but we would take shot after shot to ignore reality and live in the present.

Zero Tolerance

On the way home, Nathan did something I would never have thought he would do. This is when the abuse became more physical. I knew he had zero tolerance, but I did not think he would go that far. A friend of mine Facetimed me advising he had sent a package. It was basketballs for a basketball camp I was hosting in my community. He sent them to support me because he loved what I was doing with the kids in my community. When I hung up the phone, Nathan SNAPPED! Out of nowhere, he punched me repeatedly in my head and demanded I get out of the vehicle while it was moving. It happened so quickly; I could not believe he put his hands on me. Nathan pulled over and forced me out of the car. He yelled, shouted, and reached for his gun. He screamed, "Get out of my car; that is the same guy you are texting." I didn't understand what he was talking about. He pushed me out of the vehicle, ran over my leg, and drove off. I am on the side of the interstate, laying in the grass in shock, and holding my leg. I reached for my phone and realized it was left in the vehicle. I remember laying there, having thoughts to myself on how I was going to get home with a bruised leg. I am thankful that my leg was not broken.

Minutes later, he reverses the vehicle, pulls up to where I am, and demands I get in the car. At this time, I refused. He acted like he was reaching for his gun again. I hopped back in the vehicle to obey what he was saying. Once in the car, he drove extremely fast because he was upset. I felt as if I was looking at a demon. Every time I made eye contact with him, it made him even angrier. There were more hard hits toward my head. He spazzed before my eyes. He drove to a side street; it was like he knew this street was there. Each side of the street had swamps. Nathan commented, "I should kill you and leave you in the swamp." At that moment, I hopped out of the car and started running.

There was an older house across the street; it was the only house on the block. I saw an older couple looking out of their window. I began to stare at them, and I knew they saw the fear in my eyes and the confusion. Nathan forced me back into the car. I remember pulling the mirror down and immediately fell into tears. My lip was busted, blood was all over my face, and a scratch on my nose. I only saw stuff like this on TV, and I am bruised and abused, not Kyra King. A helicopter was in the area and Nathan felt like that couple had called the police. He goes on to say, "If we get pulled over, I am going to kill the officer, you, and then myself." Minutes later, he was ok again, and we rode the rest of the way home in silence.

Labor Pains

Once we arrived in Atlanta, my son's father was waiting at my apartment with my son. He had a key to my apartment for when he would bring my son home, so he and my son would not have to sit in the car until I arrived. My son's father lives in North, GA. We were co-parenting and had a good relationship. He is a good father and I respect him for that. He never abandoned our son and was always there when our baby boy needed anything. I was afraid to tell Nathan my child's father was inside my apartment. I did not want him to try to come in when he dropped me off because I knew he would not understand. It would look like I wanted my cake and ice cream in Nathan's eyes. I wanted to lie down, call my family, and go to the hospital.

My son's father knew something odd was going on. I didn't want him in my business, so I made him leave when he asked if I needed help. Mentally, I was done. I knew Nathan was not the guy for me. He turned into an animal after being dishonest about his whole life, your children, for God's sake. Over the next few days, I suffered from not wanting to be alone, and I forgave him for his wrongdoing. The vibe was different.

He invited me over for seafood. He knew my son and I loved seafood. He fixed an entire crab boil. Moments later, his sister brought a baby girl downstairs. It is his daughter, the youngest one, with Raegan. He did not tell me she was there. Not that I had a problem. Then he says, "Raegan is having a baby and wanted me to watch her." I wondered how he could make seafood bowls for your girlfriend and her child while the mother of your child is in labor. Many thoughts ran through my mind. I did not know what to think. Raegan was calling him, but she appeared calm and happy. She was not upset; she was making sure Nathan got the baby's food and snacks from Walmart, since he was keeping her until she got out of the hospital. At this point, I thought everybody was weird, including me. Situations like these were unheard of, not normal. This was his seventh child. I was over it and hauling around. I had gotten so used to his company that I honestly felt addicted. I knew I wasn't myself at all. I did not know where to begin to move on. I knew moving on would hurt.

Down and Out

Nathan and I were in the process of buying an investment condo downtown to build passive income. However, I was not excited to do anything with him anymore. I was torn between my broken heart and the betrayal. It was time to separate. Nathan began asking me to loan him four thousand dollars because he was "down and out." He mentioned he needed the money to put down on the condo because I was his girl and was supposed to be there for him. I continued to tell him no until we broke up and officially separated. I called to check on him from time to time and every call would be ignored. He was really mad that I did not loan him the money and that I canceled our "plans." He even ended up changing his number. At that time, I began to get distant and heal. I began traveling again and enjoying my life, attempting to erase the memories I had with Nathan.

Losing Myself

My sister Kenya saw that I was losing myself. We are seven years apart. Our relationship is different, she is a cool big sister, but she enjoys playing my second mom more. She doesn't get involved in my business, but when it is time for her to be a big sister, she carries the title well. My sister knew

I was at rock bottom. It was crazy because she didn't know what was happening, but she knew I was off. She invited me to a church conference, and it changed my life. I later joined the church and we both went faithfully every Sunday. When I started grad school, my mind was occupied with being a mommy, a student, and spending more time with my family. I was finally back in a happy place and not depending on a man for a good time or for me to feel good.

I looked on his baby mom's Instagram page from time to time to see what he was up to or what he was doing, really seeing if they had gotten back together. At times, she would post him spending time with the kids, but it was never consistent, so I knew they were not back together officially. For all I know, I thought the man was trying to be a better father. It gave me peace that maybe he was not a terrible person after all, but it gave me validation to continue to move on. I spent time with friends to continue getting my mind off him, focusing on what I wanted to accomplish in 2020.

PRAYER FOR HEALING

Dear God,

I come to You seeking Your healing and comfort. Lord, I feel overwhelmed by my circumstances and struggle to find hope and joy in my life. I ask that You lift me up and give me the strength to overcome this darkness.

Please help me focus on Your goodness and promises and find peace in Your presence. I know that You are greater than any challenge I may face and that with Your help, I can overcome any difficult situation.

I trust in Your healing power, and I believe You will help me find joy and hope again.

In Jesus' name, Amen.

Chapter 4

Hoovering

CHAPTER 4

HOOVERING

Hoovering Stage is when the Narcissist wants you back to abuse you again. At this stage, they have run out of supply from another relationship and are looking to benefit off you again to survive and feel important. This stage is when you are convinced back into the relationship and brainwashed on the original reason why you left.

The Pandemic of 2020

March 2020, I am still in grad school, working, and in a good space. However, that changed when one day I received an email from Nathan. It read, "Hey Kyra, I am sorry for how we ended." I know I did not properly give you the closure you deserved, but I wanted to say I am sorry." I could not believe it was him. He ghosted me and changed his number. All I wanted was a genuine apology for all he had done, and there it was. I responded that I forgave him and for him to call me. He called later that day; we caught up on missed time. He was doing better. He had gotten promoted to finance manager and had moved to Buckhead in a condo. He stated, there was a lot going on with him, I didn't deserve him being dishonest and that he wanted us to be cool.

I was curious to see if he had changed because I still loved him. I told him we could catch up over the weekend since we both worked long hours during the week. The weekend came and he invited me over. I arrived and the condo was beautiful. He let me through the gate, and I parked. When I saw him, my heart dropped like it was the first time we ever met. I had butterflies all over again, he hugged me, and my body was frozen. We get in the elevator and we stare at each other and smile continuously. It's like our eyes were speaking, saying, "I missed you and I missed you too." I was so happy to see him, it's like I had forgotten about everything.

We get to his floor, and we enter the condo. He has made dinner, candles are lit, and he gives me a tour. It was so nice. There was plenty of open space, a beautiful view, the house was sparkling clean, his bed was made up, and the house smelled good. Even the bathroom had a TV in it. The first thing I thought about was that I could not wait to take a bubble bath and watch TV in there. We ate, chilled, laughed, and talked about things we had going on. When I got home, I thought about him all night. It was like I had forgotten the reason we initially broke up.

I began to go over there every day. After some time, he gave me a key to the condo. Things between us would be better this time around. I can trust him; I have a key to his place, which means he trusts me to be here alone. He must not be hiding anything from me. I was having a good time, but I told myself not to commit to anything serious with him. Well, that lasted about two weeks, and we were back together. I felt like it was our new beginning. We spent so much time together and could not keep our hands off each other. The pandemic was going on, my son's daycare was closed, and he was with his dad. I was kid free and relaxed.

We were like two teenage kids in love, taking more road trips during the pandemic and enjoying life. I even took him to my hometown in Chicago and visited my grandfather's church and house he built with his bare hands. This visit was meaningful because I was close to my grandfather, who passed away in 2015. My baby boy is named after him. During my college days, my grandfather would sit on the phone with me all day. His memory wasn't the best, but he knew it was me every time I called, and we would talk for hours.

Everything was going so well in our relationship and my family loved him. We decided to take a road trip to South Florida for my birthday. One of my friends and her boyfriend joined us. Once we arrived, he played all our favorite songs, and then it happened. I'll Be Loving you Forever by Damage starts playing. Nathan gets down on one knee and pulls a beautiful ring out of his pocket. I mean, BEAUTIFUL. I couldn't believe this was happening. He really loves me. I got the ring. He proposed so fast that my friend was not paying attention and she did not record. Even though I was happy, I would have liked a proposal that included my family. He did not even ask my dad for my hand. We walked to the beach right after and he played, "He proposed," by Kelly Price on his speaker. We were in love; it was us forever.

Weak Female

We are back home, and I had this big diamond ring on my hand, but I am also saddened because I am making my appointment to terminate another pregnancy. I am embarrassed because the clinic must know me by name by now. I remember going in there and the walls felt like they were folding in on me. The sad part is that I knew better. As I prayed, I asked God for forgiveness, begging Him not to judge my actions but rather my heart. I was mad because I had finally found the man of my dreams, but he had so much baggage. It was not fair to me. I took a lot of my anger out on him. I wanted to punish him for not waiting for me and for making so many careless decisions. The space I was in was unhealthy and I never imagined myself being there ever in life and yet here I was. I felt like a total weak female and totally disconnected from God.

After I had the procedure, I had to be on bed rest. I spent those days at my house because I was emotionally drained and needed to be alone. He would text me saying I should be ashamed of how many times I kept getting rid of his babies. He also said I needed to pray because I was going to hell. Part of me felt like he was right. I prayed, but I also blamed him for being so reckless. I also was mad at myself for being so careless.

I healed and I went back to the condo to stay with him (crazy, I know). While he was at the gym, he left his laptop open, and I browsed through his Facebook messages. He sent money to a woman in exchange for naked videos. I was pissed because this was during the time I was home healing. I was mad, but I knew I wasn't going anywhere.

I started looking for birth control options. I was so afraid of birth control, because I saw how it negatively impacted so many of my friends, by gaining weight or losing hair on their heads. I did not care anymore. I was getting on it because I could not take another risk, I could not break my promise to God. I promised I would not do that again. It is now November. I spent Thanksgiving with his family. His mom cooked and we later went to his cousin's house, another good time.

The Mom

I never got a good vibe from his mother. The first time I met her, I knew she was not a good person. Nathan told me she was a prophet. I do not like questioning God's people or talking down upon them, but that lady was not a prophet. To be honest, I knew she was the complete opposite, wicked. She treated his twin sisters like puppets; they are thirty years old, but they move like ten-year-olds. No voice of their own, they do as their mother says. They live with her, they moved five times in the same year as if they move every time, they are about to get evicted. I thought maybe they were on section 8 because Nathan told me they grew up poor. He was like the man in their little family, his mom's man too. Whenever I came around his mom, she disturbed my spirit and rubbed me the wrong way. This bothered me because I get along with everybody, especially older people. I thought it was odd for a God-fearing woman like herself to side-eye me and not make me feel welcome.

She had a boutique, and, in the back, she would host her church service. She had about two members and the rest were her sons and their girlfriends, including me. You could tell they brought every girl they dated to church to give their mom an offering. I never gave an offering. It took only a few times for me to attend to catch on to how she ran her service.

During one service, she tried to pray for me. As she reached for my hands, I began to shake uncontrollably. My hands were shaking nonstop to the point it scared her. She yelled, "Whew Lord, I am not going to touch you, I am not going to pray for you, you are making me nervous." At that moment, I knew I was right about her. I knew I was the woman of God in the room and God was protecting me from the real demon. She called me a demon and said the reason I was shaking was because of a demon I had on me. I said to myself if you feel I have a demon in me why not pray for me then? Why run from me? When you have the power to rebuke this "demon." The Bible states, "Resist the devil and he will flee from you (James 4:7)." There was nowhere in the Bible that stated the Lord our God flees from the devil. Why did she flee from me? I knew then she was wicked, taking the two older women who attended the church's money to survive and brainwashing them, telling them she was a prophet.

How could you be so good of a prophet for over 20 years with no members? No name for your church. The same two members who have been attending for twenty years, are your friends. How could you be a prophet when your church has not grown at all? There is no children's ministry or kids to teach the Word to besides your grandchildren. How could you be a woman of God, knowing your sons are out here making so many babies with different women and being abusive? How could you be a woman of God when you have grandchildren you do not even call and check up on, knowing they exist? How could you?

Nathan wanted me to know that his mom was a prophet. She would repeat conversations in service that Nathan and I previously had to try to convince me that she was gifted. I never went for it. I came from a real praying family. Playing with God and using His Word to manipulate people was something we did not do. The vibe was never pleasant when she came around. I would be ready for her and the sisters to leave when they came over. I did not want her to touch my son at all. She was weird and never cared anyway, so we were good on that end. Nathan's mom had no high school education or college. She was a halfway entrepreneur with her boutique, which means I knew how she was surviving, off her son and her "church."

I knew Nathan was messed up mentally from his mom. I knew she was a narcissistic mom who manipulated her children and broke them down mentally. She screwed them up and still is. She was not a loving mother at all. I could tell her love was based on survival, especially when it came to Nathan. He was the breadwinner, the favorite.

Moving On

Back to looking for the most effective birth control option for me. I called multiple doctors and got the background on all of them. I even called a few people to get their advice on what was the best one to try. I came down to having the surgery where they place a chip inside of you to prevent you from conceiving for five or ten years. I thought this was the perfect option. However, when I went for my appointment to get the surgery, they advised me that my hormone count was too high due to the recent abortion. I needed to wait a few more weeks to make sure I was not pregnant. They told me to come back on December 8, 2020, to get the surgery.

Well, the day came, and I was on the way there on the phone with Nathan. I reminded him of my appointment, and he stated, *"I don't know why you are going bae; you are already pregnant."* I responded, *"Please do not say that because I am not playing."* He says, *"You are."* I take him seriously at this point and go to the nearest drug store. I picked up a pregnancy test and parked at a Wendy's that was nearby. I then called a family friend and told her about the conversation. She stayed on the phone while I went inside Wendy's to take the test.

Yes, there were two lines. I was pregnant AGAIN. I sat in my car and cried because I knew I was not going back to that clinic. I knew it was finally time to lay in the bed that I made. I knew it was time to stop being selfish and to do the right thing. I called him back and told him he was right and that I was keeping this one. He was totally fine with it; the man was more excited than me. The pregnancy hormones kicked in and as he would say my attitude began to get bad. I was always tripping, taking the excitement out of the pregnancy. I was excited but also felt set up. I wanted everything to go right. I wanted to at least enjoy a wedding and being married for a year without a newborn. I was sad because none of that was going to happen. Here it is: we are preparing for a new child when we already have enough. My attitude changed. I hated him, and he felt it.

New Home 2020

We closed on our home in the beginning of December. I was upset about that because I covered the closing costs. We were supposed to go half, but Nathan ended up owing somebody money right before we closed, so I had to cover the amount plus more. Looking back, that was probably a lie too. I'm sure he pocketed that. The loan was in his name, and I was waiting to go on once we were married to be placed on the deed. The attorney's office we went through had strict rules. Literally, the attorney would not allow me to sign, unless we provided a marriage certificate.

We are in our new home, and it is beautiful. Nathan covered the majority of the furniture. It was like he was trying to make up for slacking on his end of the closing. We moved everything in, just us two and were excited doing so. Once we were in, Nathan purchased a grand piano and did the marble floors in our dining room. The house was beautiful, for it being our first time owning a home. We were excited to host Christmas at our home. His family came to town. He had an aunty I fell in love with. She was the complete opposite of his mom. She thought she was weird too and overly "Christian." In other words, faking the funk. We were happy to be in a new home. His three children are over. These are the three children he had with his first child's mother. The only genuine relationship he had. These are the children his mother shows the most consistent love to.

Then there's Kairo. This little girl is the most beautiful little girl you will ever see, inside and out. Kairo is Nathan's fifth child. You can call her second favorite. Nathan spends time with Kairo here and there, but consistently Facetimes her, even when she lives in the same city. Dillon is the fourth born, but Nathan has not seen him or Dillon's mom in years, he pays her monthly. She lives in Columbus, Georgia. Then there's Raegan, she has two little girls. One is the same age as Kairo, and the other is a year younger. I always had a soft spot for Raegan because she told me the truth about Nathan. Also, I knew deep down she was not crazy for no reason, I knew it had to be more to the story but could not figure it out due to Raegan also acting too crazy at times, like making fake police reports to get our attention.

For Christmas, we had the first three at our house. We kept them for about two weeks while their mom worked.

It's crazy because Nathan lied about how this girl acted too, and now she is a millionaire. She never was lazy like he claimed she was. She owns a very successful tax firm in Atlanta. I could tell she raised them correctly; they were polite and soft spoken. She had another daughter Nathan claimed due to raising her since she was a baby. She was also there all the time. He spent more time doing for her than for his own blood. Christmas went well. I made sure all the kids got gifts and Nathan gave cash and ear pods. Things were looking and feeling good. After we finished exchanging gifts with the kids, we walked outside to the garage. There it was a 2021 Black Audi A5, with a red bow on the front.

It was my Christmas gift from Nathan. His smile was from ear to ear, and so was mine. I complained all year about how I wanted a new car, and he finally blessed me with one. I am now riding in style. You could not tell me anything. Our Christmas was complete. I was happy! At times I could be materialistic and blinded by gifts. Today, none of that matters and it no longer excites me. I don't care about the gifts, but how you treat me and how you make me feel. There comes a time when you realize that nothing materialistic matters.

January 2021

We are getting settled into the home and I am now about two months pregnant. Nathan and I decided to push our wedding date up so that our child would be welcomed in the family. We decided to do the craziest thing. We began to plan our wedding for the month of March - only two months away. It had to be in March because I also did not want to be too big in my dress. My family is creative, so once I made the phone calls, everybody began planning. I knew my family was wondering what in the world is this girl doing. I didn't care. I had the attitude that you would either get on board or move along. It did not make any difference, but surprisingly, they were so supportive and did not even question it. Some of my aunts and uncles have not even met him because they live in Chicago, but they did not care. They knew I was getting married; I was happy, and I asked them to be there. My cousin started gathering and making decorations. My creative aunt began to make my dress. My sisters and cousins were my bridesmaids, and they started ordering dresses. Nathan got his boys on board. Wedding planning was in full effect. Nathan and I went to the court to apply for our marriage license but ended up signing the wrong paperwork and had to reschedule (God's protection).

It is now late January; the relationship is still going, but we began to argue here and there. Fights are still happening; he is still being abusive, and I could hardly go anywhere. I do not even remember half of the arguments, but I know it caused him to stay away from home some nights. He still had the condo in Buckhead, due to the lease not being up until the following month. Whenever we argue, he would stay there. I pulled up in the middle of the night to make sure he was there, and he was. Not one time did I think another woman could be too. As soon as I saw his vehicle, I was content and drove back home. I did not trip too much on him staying at the condo because at times I wanted the bed to myself. I too needed space and I was tired of fighting and getting choked out over absolutely nothing. During this time, I was begging God to end the relationship because I did not have the strength to. I knew I needed help; I can admit I was weak.

PRAYER FOR STRENGTH

Dear Lord,

I come to You in a time of uncertainty and heartache, seeking Your guidance and strength. Lord, I ask for Your courage and wisdom to do what is right for me. Please help me to let go of any fears or doubts, and to trust in Your plan for my life. Please be with me as I make difficult decisions and give me the strength to follow through with it. Please guide me on a path that leads to healing and wholeness.

Thank you for Your love, grace, and for always being there for me. I trust in Your unfailing love, and I believe that You will help me to find peace and joy in my life once again.

In Jesus' name, Amen.

CHAPTER 5

DISCARD

CHAPTER 5

DISCARD

The Discard Stage is when you are totally abandoned by the Narcissist. You now know they never loved you and everything was a lie. You realize the whole relationship was for their benefit. They never were into you and the relationship was planned before they met you. They had it all planned out to manipulate and abuse you from day one.

Financial Abuse

Now starts the financial abuse. I was driving to work, and I received a phone call from my car financing company. The phone call advised me that I was late on my car note and I needed to pay the past due amount of $800 plus the late fees. I was lost because I knew I did not have a car note, let alone a late payment. The information was not adding up though. They mentioned that I took out a loan at the beginning of the month with them for a 2021 Dodge Ram Truck. I knew that was not correct, because I did not have a 2021 Dodge Ram Truck. I had a 2019 Dodge Ram Truck that Nathan put in my name and himself as the cosigner. At least that's what I thought was going on.

He mentioned he was putting a truck in my name because he had given his other car to his mom and now needed one. He stated he could get it, but his credit was tied up with getting the house and the Audi, so I agreed. Nathan mentioned the truck was a 2019 Dodge Ram Truck, priced at $25,000. I was ok with that because $25,000 was not that much to me. I had zero debt, but I was willing to take on the loan due to him being the cosigner and the price was not that high. When they called me, I was confused because I knew we had a truck, but the information did not add up. In addition, our loan was with Associated Credit Union. I knew this because I was paying for it. At that time, I pulled up my app to see what loan I exactly was paying on, and it was a 2019 Chrysler 300. There was no sign of a truck anywhere. I knew then, they were right, and that Nathan had misled me on the information. He worked at the dealership, so I trusted him.

I called them back and asked for a copy of the loan application. There it was, Nathan had forged my signature on the loan and purchased a 2021 Dodge Ram Truck. He lied his way into purchasing two separate vehicles in my name on the same day, putting me approximately $100,000 in debt. I was devastated! I was angry!

At this time, the wedding venue was paid for, the decorations and dress were made, and the invites were sent out to our family and friends. Plus, I still loved him. I wanted to get married for my daughter and I thought maybe I could look past on why he had to lie to me to purchase the vehicles. However, I was pissed because I went from no debt to debt. The truck was in our driveway. I started to question him more. I asked Nathan if this is the truck, where is the Chrysler? He responds, *"I rented it out to one of my partners."* It is like everything he was saying was pissing me off even more. How could he be so stupid? If anything happens in that car, I will be held accountable.

How could he not know that? He stressed that he was the cosigner on the car and that he knew the guy well. Here I am, pregnant, getting married in two months, and I am angry that he misled me. My emotions at this time were beyond me. I knew I could not marry this man. It was like I was signing to death row. The manipulation was so real, it came naturally for him to smooth things over and move past issues we needed to address.

We got over it, or at least he thought we did. However, it still sat in the back of my mind, along with other things including him having seven kids and four baby mamas. It was like he was adding to my hate list. My attitude showed I was not happy the majority of the time and was trying to cover it up with the love I had for him. I knew I was financially smarter than him and I had a better understanding of what wealth was than him. He could go to the mall and purchase a five-hundred-dollar outfit, while I would have put that same five hundred dollars in a savings account or into my investment account.

Neither here nor there, we had a wedding to get ready for and I had a job interview I needed to land. This was due to my current job wanting me to sit out because of my pregnancy and I was looked at as a liability. My interview was at the courthouse because this is where all the government offices are. I wanted to get the job because it was an office position. It was perfect for me to relax, enjoy my pregnancy, and GET PAID. I told Nathan about it, and he was not supportive at all. He did not want me to work there. Nathan wanted me to stay home because his cousin used to work in one of the offices. He told him everybody sleeps with each other up there, it is like a high school. He then went on to say that I am tired of you working around men.

This began to stress me out because I wanted the position, but I did not want to upset him. I was confused on why he was so serious about me not taking the position. Why wasn't he happy for me? I was only interviewing because I was pregnant. I took the interview anyway and passed. The department I interviewed with was phenomenal. I fell in love with the whole staff. The supervisor was an older lady, and she was sweet as pie. I could tell she had the glory of God written all over her. Yes, I took the job, but I did not tell him. I hid it for weeks. My start date was in February, so I felt I had time to tell him.

The Turning Point

In February 2021, things took a turn for the worse in the household. It was the worst month of my life. Yes, the fights are still happening because this man's insecurities were worse than a woman's. I was pregnant and still getting abused because I wanted to keep my male friends who had been in my life for years.

A few weeks later, we were getting closer to his oldest daughter's birthday. I woke up and bought her a cake, and a Jordan outfit with a pair of Jordan shoes. She was so sweet and extremely grateful. His mom and sisters came over later in the day, brought ice cream and gifts for her. She was so happy! They sang Happy Birthday and spent some time together. I was not feeling well that day. My head was pounding, but I did not want to be anti-social, so I came downstairs to be engaged. When Nathan's mom was leaving that night, she called me Kyla. She always pronounced my name wrong when I knew for a fact, she knew my name and how it was pronounced. Why? Because Nathan corrected her not once but twice. A couple of days later, Nathan and I argued again. We argued because I looked through his phone and saw he sent money to Raegan's oldest daughter (not his daughter), money for her birthday. I was upset because here it is I cannot have any male friends, cannot take job opportunities because of his insecurities but he could give his baby mama's daughter birthday gifts. I felt there should be zero tolerance across the board. If I sent my child's father's other son birthday money, I would have gotten cursed and choked out.

Nathan and I began to get distant. He was not the same, I felt it. I knew something was off. He was not mentally there anymore, and neither was I. He texted me and said, "*My mom is starting not to like you, she did not like how you weren't singing happy birthday to your supposedly stepdaughter.*" His mom never liked me. She finally had an excuse she could use to explain why she didn't like me. I later voiced my concerns to Nathan about his mom.

Then I also felt that his mom probably did not say that, but that he was finding ways to argue and distance himself more. He was mad that I took the job. Ignoring him, I got up one morning, put my suit on and went to work. You could tell he was disgusted and had already begun to plan an escape route.

Every day he told me to quit, and I would not. Our mornings and nights became more and more distant. He would speak to my son and not me in the morning. He started sleeping on the couch. I felt so incomplete, stressed, and overwhelmed. Nathan was not the same. We barely kissed, had sex, or spent time together. I was dealing with knowing he put extra cars in my name, being pregnant, a wedding that was weeks away and me not wanting to quit my job. However, I knew that was the only way we would come back to being us was if I quit.

His Birthday

Nathan's birthday was at the end of the month, and I wanted to make his birthday special. For God's sake we were getting married in a week. I got one of my friends to bake his favorite cake, Red Velvet. I decorated the house and hired a saxophone player to play our wedding songs while we ate dinner. Steak and potatoes were on the menu, and I invited his best friend and his girlfriend over to join us. The night was beautiful. Nathan wanted to spend the second part of his night with his boys. I knew then that it was over.

After a beautiful night, he still did not want to spend time with me. He would rather be with his friends and leave me home alone. I was so sad, depressed, and I felt unworthy. I wanted him home so badly, but I knew I could not be selfish (Crazy mindset, I had). It was his birthday, I was pregnant, and I could not hang out like I wanted to. I let him enjoy his night. He came home the next morning.

The vibe was off, but I knew I could not trip. I wanted the wedding to be peaceful. We were supposed to sign the marriage license and I missed the appointment due to Nathan being "tied up at work." I knew then, he was serious about not wanting to get married or was trying to prove his point about me not quitting my job. We missed the appointment, and we rescheduled it again in April, which was the court's next available appointment. I was not that upset because I felt it gave us time to work on our relationship. The month was rough for us. I wanted him to know even though I took the job it was not to down his manhood. I wanted to be comfortable. I did not want to have to fully depend on him. I never depended on a man because I was not raised that way.

The wedding is getting closer. Family is flying in from Chicago, his family came up from Alabama and Columbus, Georgia. The Friday before the wedding, we argued again. I do not even remember what happened, but he did not come home that night. I was so upset; my soul was ripped out of my body because my mom and stepdad were in town and staying at my house. My mom continued to hear me get out of bed that night. It was me checking the front window to see if his car was in the driveway. I thought to myself: was he really doing this while my parents were here? Why would he do this? I was so angry. I knew the way he operated; it was a bit childish. Things we valued in my family, in his family, they could give two cents. It was getting late in the night, and I couldn't take it anymore. I got out of bed, woke my mom up and explained to her how I was feeling. I also explained to her that Nathan and I were arguing, and he wasn't coming home. My mom held me while sitting on the couch and I broke out in tears. I felt her heart breaking for me. She stated, *"Please do not do this, if you do not want to."* All night it was like my heart knew something was not right and he was doing something, to even be that bold to pull that move on the weekend of our wedding.

I felt like I had lost him at that moment. I lost myself. I knew our relationship was over. He was so different towards me. No kisses, no hugs, no affection and all our dates and spontaneous trips had ended. Was he really that mad that I did not quit my job? Was my attitude really that bad? I began to question if I was making the right choice in marrying him. I was about to walk down the aisle to this man; I needed that spark to reappear, and I mean fast.

We had rehearsal dinner at our home the next day. I felt better seeing our families dance and laugh together. Nathan arrives and he grabs and hugs me. I asked him why he did not come home, that he knew my mom was here regardless of whether we argued or not. I then asked him what he did last night. He responded, *"I was at the condo,"* but there was a hesitation in his voice. He sounded more guilty than he looked. My heart dropped again. I was not his precious jewel anymore. The feeling was different. I wanted to jump on a plane and go far away. I was not happy; this felt like the worst time of my life. It was hard for me because I knew better but for the life of me, I could not get it together and do better. I was still forcing the relationship; I knew moving on would hurt more.

It was not the time to spark another argument, so I swallowed it and headed back downstairs to enjoy the family. I knew in my heart that the tears I cried the night before were for a reason, like my soul was talking to me. However, I looked past it once we both were enjoying the family. His mom and sisters showed up and met my mom and sisters. The vibe was not as weird as I imagined it would be. I was happy his mom was acting normal.

WEDDING DAY MARCH 7, 2021

Today is the big day. I was more nervous than excited. It did not feel right. I did not know whether the feeling was still genuine, or we were doing this to get it over with. I was caught up in what Nathan could be thinking, hoping he still loved me, because I still loved him. I figured that he must love me because we are here now, it is our day. I was hoping he would think I was more beautiful today than on any other day. I wanted him to be proud that I was becoming his wife.

Here it is time for me to meet my fiancé at the altar. My dad is proud to walk me down. He is filled with emotions and happiness. It was all in his eyes and in his smile. Sort of how I expected Nathan to look at me. I am now walking down the aisle and I see Nathan. He is smiling from ear to ear with his dimples showing. However, there were no tears or watery eyes. It was a happy, but blank look. While walking down the aisle, I fought the voices in my head telling me to turn around. I thought it was me being nervous and anxious. Another scripture is, "Be anxious for nothing." (Philippians 4:6-7 KJV) I knew it was not right, but I went against the force again. The voices were getting louder and louder.

I am at the altar and the pastor asks everyone to be seated. I am so nervous and shaking. Nathan is staring at me with a smile, I smiled back. Maybe, we were good, maybe we were not. I began to think everything was ok and calmed down. The pastor says his spill and now we are saying our vows. His groomsmen were so goofy throughout the ceremony. It was getting to me a little because they would laugh when we would stumble over our words after repeating the pastor. The best man forgot to take the tag of the ring, which again they all thought was funny. My sister had to assist with getting the tag detached to go on with the ceremony. Yes, I giggled, but I was not in a playing mood.

It is now the end of the ceremony, and the pastor pronounces us Mr. & Mrs. Birks. In the middle of him announcing us, the groomsmen shouted out, "Mrs. King." As if Nathan was taking my last name. Another moment, I was not in the mood to play. It was like they had never been anywhere. The only one who knew how to act was my male cousin, whom Nathan had gotten cool with. He giggled, but not to draw attention.

We are now downstairs taking pictures. Everyone looks so nice. Our venue was on a golf course. The view was breathtaking, it was an amazing day. Nathan didn't have many words to say. I could tell we were still not there. There were a few moments when I felt special and beautiful, but I mostly felt blank. It was his silence that bothered me. He was not his silly self that day. It was more of a vibe that he wanted to get over with. He was on his phone and at times not attentive. He would then kiss my forehead and ask me what my last name was, with a smile. He could see the sadness in my eyes but wanted to make me smile for the moment. We are done taking our pictures and he goes to talk to his guys while I went to mingle with family.

At that time, his mom walks up to me as if she were in a rush and states, *"Hi Kyra, (She got my name right this time.), you look so beautiful, I am about to get ready to go because I have a Life Course class to teach at 6pm."* At that moment, my heart dropped to the floor. My eyes were filled with tears, but I did not let them fall down my face. I was not about to let this woman ruin the only time I had my makeup done. I was so upset. How could she leave her son's wedding to go teach a class? She then went to tell my mom and my family the same thing and of course everyone was looking confused, including Nathan. I said to myself again, this is the reason why her son is so screwed up. What kind of mother leaves her son's wedding and then makes an excuse that was piss poor? She knew her son was getting married on this exact day and she scheduled a class? I wanted to dance at the reception. I wanted her to stay, give a speech, and most importantly dance with her son. None of that happened. His grandmother on his father's side had to dance with him.

Nathan's father's side seems a bit more normal. They were fun and like my family. They knew how to dress for a wedding. The family was not weird or anti-social. The complete opposite, they were happy for us and willing to get to know and meet my family. Everybody wanted to have a good time. His mom and sisters had left. I didn't even see his sisters at the wedding. They didn't congratulate us or speak to us at all. They were like the three trio, riding together and leaving together. We did not let that stop our day, we moved on to the reception.

Nathan was upset that my son's godfather was there, an innocent friend. Earlier in the year at an event I held, they got into an altercation. Nathan told Terrance, my son's Godfather, that he was responsible for me now and I did not need any brother figures in my life. He made Terrance feel uneasy, but Terrance held his tongue out of respect for me. Terrance was about to say something, but then looked at me and saw the fear in my eyes for him not to retaliate. That day did not end well. Nathan slapped me in the face once we were in the car out of nowhere and stated, *"That dude like you, I am not stupid."*

An old friend of mine heard us arguing after the event and came to our condo to check on me. When she arrived, she witnessed my things being thrown everywhere and Nathan going crazy, holding his gun. Trying to protect me, she attempts to check Nathan physically and he reacts by putting his hands on her. She is screaming and demanding I leave with her. Again I did not listen, I stayed. I was more embarrassed because it was hurtful to see him touch my friend, but more hurtful for her to know I was being abused. I always painted a perfect picture of my relationship to my family and friends. No one knew I was depressed and being abused. I kept everything from everybody. The abuse became my normal and I would sit there in silence as he would yell and get angry. A lot of anger was built up inside me, and sometimes I would fight back, but it made it worse.

I knew he was upset about Terrance being at the wedding. I never told him he was on the guest list, both he and his mom were. This guy has been in my life, accepted to be in my son's life, and has been there for me in many ways. We had an innocent friendship and Nathan wanted me to cut him off due to his insecurities. I did not think that was fair. I had already cut off my childhood friend and guys who were like brothers to me.

Nathan made a comment, *"Why is he here? Did you run it by me if he could come?"* I began to get emotional. I started thinking to myself how you could say anything to me when your own mother walked out on your big day, but you are checking me about a genuine friend who is still here for the both of us. How dare you? Terrance spoke to Nathan, but we all could see it was a dry hey and he was still not ready to accept Terrance in my life as one of my male friends. I was over it; Nathan began to check his phone more throughout the reception. It was making me mad because at this current moment what can be more important than your wedding? Maybe, he was on social media recording, but I knew that was not it. Later that night, I looked and there were no videos posted of the wedding. The wedding is coming to an end and our guests are ready to walk us out. Everyone grabs their fire sticks and heads outside; they cheer us on to our car and we sit there because Nathan is too drunk to drive. Mind you, I am sober due to a baby bump. I look out to my family, and they are all so happy and tipsy. My family laughed and was trying to see where the after party was. Everybody decided to hang out at my cousin Monica's house. She cooked a seafood dinner, and they all took more shots and drank more. I drove back to the hotel because Nathan was out of it at this point.

The next morning, he had to go to work. We rescheduled our honeymoon trip to Las Vegas due to how much we were arguing and that I was pregnant and was not going to have much fun. We wake up and I take Nathan home to get dressed for work. He wanted to travel to Mississippi with the wedding gifts we received. We received a good amount of money from the wedding. We drove to Mississippi, got a nice room and gambled all night. We lost all of it. My mood began to change again. It was like I was already thinking of an escape route, but still wanted to fight for our marriage, relationship or whatever it was. I slept the whole ride back home the following morning. Nathan went on to work, and I went home to enjoy my last day off before returning to work.

The Week After the Wedding

I return to work and again the conversation is short. He has that look on his face like he did all last month about me starting the job. I got to work, and I received a text from him that said, *"I thought you said you were going to be working from home?"* Another text came in and it stated, *"If you do not quit, I do not want you or the baby."* I responded, trying to keep the peace as hard as I could and it did not work, so I snapped. I was upset because what else did I have to do to prove I loved him? I got married in spite of all the red flags and I was now four months pregnant with our child. Why was he so worried about the next man? His response came off premeditated. He responded saying he was tired of arguing and that he was about to explode, and I could not see it. His next line stated, he could not take it anymore and that he was out because I was ungrateful for everything he did for me.

I responded apologizing, but still trying to get him to understand that we should not be arguing over me wanting to keep a job. I was frustrated because he wanted me to quit and stay home full time. The man was so manipulative, I was even thinking of quitting to keep the peace. Nathan was beginning to convince me that the new owners at his job had made him Director. This meant that he could continue to hold down the house because he was making more money. I knew he was lying, and that was one reason I did not quit. I had enough sense to know that no new owners would come into the company and make anyone from the old staff the boss. Why would they do that? Plus, one day I saw a business card in his truck that listed another dealership. It was the General Manager's business card. Why would he have this? He was looking for a new job due to his old dealership having new owners take over and probably not taking on the old staff.

I was confused as to why he could not just tell me that. Why did he feel like he had to lie about his income? I have never been the gold digger type or came across that way. Honestly, I am the complete opposite. I wanted him to be honest and if he knew he was looking for another job, why was he trying to get me to quit mine? I rode past the dealership and I saw he had the business card from, and his truck was parked there for weeks during the day. I knew he had started working there for sure. We still argued at home back and forth about my job. There were more physical fights, which caused more holes in the wall. This man did not even care that I was pregnant with his child, I got choked out even more.

One day I came home and all of Nathan's things were gone. I mean not a shoe in the house. He had taken his basketball he used at the gym, protein shakes, TV out of the den, and the bed out of the guest room. My heart was shattered, it was broken. At that moment, it was like a light bulb instantly came on for me. Throughout the whole relationship, I was blinded by the obvious and ignored family, friends, and red flags. No one could get me to change my mind about him, even knowing I was in an unhealthy relationship.

Losing my Mind

I sat in my bed that night in silence. I did not eat. I could feel my daughter kicking me lightly, she was still in the growing phase. My son begged me to feed him. It felt like I wasn't there. I heard my son, and I felt my daughter, but I was literally in a space where I had zoned out and could not move. When I finally came back to my senses, it was about eleven at night. My son was laying on my lap with honey bun wrappers everywhere that he had gotten himself out of the pantry, the house was mostly pitch black. I felt terrible. I knew I was losing my mind to the point I didn't even make sure my son ate before bed. All I remember was him saying he wanted food and he looked at me and stated, *"Mommy where is all of our stuff? Who took our TV? Where is Nathan?"* Mind you, my son is four years old, and he loved Nathan. He loved it when he put together all his toys and played with him. That was his best friend.

I did not have an answer. I sat there for hours zoned out. All types of thoughts were running through my head. I felt like I was in jail mentally. Nathan had cameras in the inside of the house that only he had access to. I am pregnant and alone with $100,000 in debt that he put me in. More thoughts: Is it over for real this time? No, it cannot be, we had a whole wedding. It is over because everything of his is gone, there was no trace of him. It was like he had vanished. I did not sleep or eat at all that night. I had thoughts to end my life, but knew nothing good would come from that from a spiritual perspective and how selfish would that be for my kids? The pain was so intense that I wanted it all to end. I did not want to feel the pain or face the embarrassment.

I barely could get up for work, so I called off. I took my son to school, and I went back and laid in bed the whole day. I didn't eat and I felt my daughter kicking and I did not care. My oldest sister brought me meals and left them at my front door. I did not want to get up, I did not want to do anything. It was like I was waiting on God to take us all. I called and texted Nathan non-stop and all I got was short answers and being left on read. He responded once and said, *"I told you I was leaving, if you did not quit like I told you to."* It was over, officially. He was not budging or taking accountability for anything I was saying to him. He would not answer any calls. He was gone for good this time. I wanted to scream and throw things around the house, but I did not. I knew I had to come up with a plan for me and my children. I knew I had to fight through the pain, I had to see it through. I felt so set up and like a total failure who got played twice and was now about to face embarrassment from family, friends, and myself. It was like I could see everything for what it was. I hated myself so badly, how could I be so weak and stupid? I knew better. Now, I am sitting here pregnant, with two kids, and alone.

First, I knew I had to clear my credit from those loans and clear my name. I reported fraud claims to the carriers and credit bureaus. I had to partake in police reports due to forgery. It was one of the toughest things in my life to do because I still loved and cared about Nathan. I did not want to put him in any legal trouble, but I had to think about Kyra, Grayson, and Lyric. It was so crazy because I was still not trying to ruin his life after he ruined mine.

I had to think about if I did nothing and stayed in that house, I would never be able to own anything. I would have to rent and struggle credit wise for years. That was not fair to me or my children. I began to put a shield up and went to war with the little morals I had left and was ready to fight for my kid's future. I knew this was the end for Nathan and I. At this point, I knew I would never go back or attempt this relationship again. Banks began to call me and ask me about the case. I explained to them the truth and exactly what happened. They then got their attorneys involved. This is when things became more like a movie, and it was me and God against every obstacle.

Prayer for Overcoming Obstacles

Dear God,

I come to You in a time of difficulty and challenge, seeking Your help and guidance. I know that You are a God of strength and power, and that nothing is impossible for You.

Lord, I am facing obstacles that seem impossible, and I feel overwhelmed and discouraged. However, I know that with Your help, I can overcome anything that comes my way. Please give me the courage and perseverance to face these obstacles. Help me to trust in Your plan for my life, even when things seem uncertain and difficult.

Thank you for your love, grace, and always being there for me. I trust in your unfailing love, and I know that you will help me overcome these obstacles and emerge stronger than ever.

In Jesus' name, Amen.

Chapter 6

The Battle

CHAPTER 6

THE BATTLE

This was the toughest time of my life. The banks were understanding, but you could tell they did not believe me fully. One specific bank gave me a hard time. They began to question my story over and over. They felt as though I had knowledge of him purchasing the vehicle, which I did not. Nathan misled me about all information about the banks, including the savings account I had for my son since he was a baby. They placed a hold on the account until the investigation was over. This was the 2019 Chrysler loan he had gotten from them. I went weeks fighting with the attorney and speaking up for myself. I sent him police reports and a copy of the loan application. The attorney then began to call me more often with follow ups and contacted other financial institutions who I also reported to. Those institutions realized there were over 20 cars in Nathan's name tied to them. They realized he had submitted a lot of bad deals to banks while working at the dealership. This led them to finally get in contact with the owner of the dealership, John Johnson.

Mr. Johnson called me one afternoon. I'm guessing he got my number from Nathan. The conversation went like this:

John Johnson: *Hey, is this Kyra?*

Me: *Yes.*

John Johnson: *I received a phone call advising that my dealership is being sued. What is going on?*

I began to explain to him what Nathan had done and how he misled me on information to purchase vehicles in my name.

John Johnson: *May I buy the vehicles back from you, so I will not have a bad relationship with the banks? I still have a business to run at our location in North Georgia.*

Me: *How am I going to get the vehicles back and I do not have them?*

John Johnson: *He then told me to ask Nathan for them and that once he had them in his possession, he would buy them back.*

Me: *Ok, I will. I will call you when I have both vehicles.*

Simple fix, right? It was not so easy. I began to contact Nathan more frequently asking for the vehicles. He continued to say his homeboy still had the Chrysler and that he was trying to get it back from him. I then asked for the truck he had; he did not really want to give it to me. I told him, *"If you give me the truck, then you can have the Audi back."* I asked him to leave the truck in the guest parking lot, with the keys inside and I would have my father come pick it up. Once he had it in his possession, I would give him the Audi.

I went to the condo weeks before that to see if he still lived there and if he parked the truck in the same spot and he did. There was another luxury sky rise condo in the area to look at and enjoy the view. I went during the night. When I arrived, I observed the truck parked. I then checked to see if it was unlocked, and it was. Now, I just needed the key. I discovered a female's purse with Nathan's wallet inside and there was a box of Magnum condoms open in the middle compartment, none left. I sat there for a minute and cried. I knew it was over. He had slept with somebody not even a week of walking down the aisle and saying vows. He had really moved on and had this premeditated like I assumed. When I returned to the car, I sat and looked down at my stomach and wedding ring while texting him and being emotionally destructive. His response was that he told me it was over and that he was going to call the police if I did not get out of the truck. I stayed out there all-night crying until the morning. It is now about 8:00 am, and he walks out with a female to the truck. I got out of the vehicle, yelling, and screaming at him and drove off. It was the most hurtful thing to watch.

This man really did not love me. It had to be a whole lie and now my blindfolds are removed, I'm woke. How could you move on and be laid up with a female so comfortably already? I knew then that I had made the right decision by clearing my credit and attempting to get my life back. Weeks later, I am still asking to swap vehicles, especially after seeing he had females in my vehicle. Who did he think he was? I begged him for the money he owed me, which was about $10,000 and for the vehicles. I was determined to fix my situation, fight through the pain, and move on with my life as well. I knew we were not signing the marriage certificate and that it was over. I was ok with missing another scheduled appointment at this point. Moving on hurts, but I had to do it.

An investigator from his last employer contacted me asking for his whereabouts. He stated they had fired Nathan due to him stealing down payments on car loans. He stated he had gotten my information from the home address that pulled up for Nathan. Not only did this man steal from me, but he stole from the employer. It was official; Nathan was a thief and a liar.

Entering Auto- Georgia Law Code OCGA 16-8-18

Nathan agreed to leave the vehicle parked with the keys inside. Again, I told him my father was coming to pick up the truck the next morning. The next morning comes, and my dad Facetimes me stating, the vehicle is not there. I contacted Nathan asking what happened. He acted so lost and told me to report the car stolen because he did his part by leaving the vehicle parked where I asked him to leave it. I did not waste any time and I contacted the police department and made a stolen vehicle report. Not only did I do that, but I also returned to the condo with a police officer to look at the cameras.

I could not believe he was not going to give me the truck and that he wanted me to report it stolen. The officer and I are at the condo, and we speak with the property manager. We give her the police case number, and she allows us access to surveillance. We observed Nathan leaving the truck parked at 7:00 pm. At 2:00 am we observed three vehicles pulling up in front of the truck. One guy hops out and jumps into the truck. They all pull off; the truck included.

I say to myself, he is crazy, and will go to the yard to stress me out! I contacted him and asked if he knew a tracker was on the vehicle. He helped me locate the vehicle and it is now in Tennessee. I knew he was crazy for helping me look for the vehicle knowing he had set that up.

It was like a nightmare that would not end. I had to get in contact with UCONNECT Services. It is a service that can locate your vehicle in situations like this. When I called advising I was the registered owner, they would not let me gain access because Nathan and his sister's name was on the account. This man had put this vehicle in my name but gave me no rights to it. The guy on the line advised Nathan or Michelle had to contact and locate the vehicle due to their names being on the UCONNECT account when the vehicle was purchased. He did not care if I was the registered owner. I knew the truck was in Tennessee, so I went from there and did my own investigation, trying not to over-stress myself and my unborn child. It didn't help, my daughter was sick every month and I was diagnosed with something at every doctor's visit. I felt like I was not only failing myself, but now my daughter. Her health was depending on me, and I was failing. I contacted the police department, sent them my police report from Georgia, and gave them the last address the car was located. Officers were on their way, but once they arrived, the truck was not at the address I had given them.

Days went by, I followed up with Mr. Johnson on the incident and he was appalled. I was then contacted by the police department in Tennessee and heard numerous sirens in the background. The police officer advised me they had located my vehicle by the tag and was behind the vehicle in a high-speed chase. He continued on to say there were about 50 officers behind my vehicle, but they were about to fall back so the suspects would not hurt anyone or wreck the vehicle. I agreed for them to stop the chase, it was crazy, it all felt unreal.

Hours later, he called back. The officer advised me that the suspects had ditched the car and that they had found my vehicle and were taking it to their tow yard. He stated, myself, or anyone I choose could come and obtain the vehicle with proper paperwork. I knew I was not driving to Tennessee. I was already mentally tired from the whole situation and was over it. I wanted it to end. Mr. Johnson agreed to send a tow truck to pick up the truck. He could tell in my voice that I was hurt, tired, and mentally exhausted. He later retrieved the truck and let me know he was writing me a check to pay the vehicle off. I was so happy. I felt like I had some control over something for once. I knew God still had his hands on me and He favored me. If God is for us, who can be against us? (Romans 8:31 KJV)

It was a blessing that Mr. Johnson paid the vehicle off, and it was off my credit a few weeks later. Now, I needed the Chrysler.

May 2021

I am still in the house with my son, alone and it is beginning to get unhealthy. I did not want to be there anymore. I could not sleep or eat. Nathan is now reaching back out to me more each day. He wanted me to stay. He said he was sorry and that he did not mean for me to end up hating him.

He told me that he gave me everything and it was not enough: A house, a car, fixed the house for me, and gave me a ring. It was as if he didn't know or understand, he had stolen from me to get those things. The house was purchased off his credit, but I paid the full closing cost and he never gave me his half after promising he would do so. The car he purchased was for him originally. On the back end, he was putting two vehicles in my name, and lying to me about the information. I could have bought my own car. The cars he put in my name added up to be more than the vehicle he purchased for me. The marble floors he installed in the house came from the funds of the vehicle he was renting out to his friend. I had no clue what was going on. I thought that my man loved me and he was fixing the house the way I wanted. He was making my vision his priority so we could be comfortable in our new home together. That was not what was going on. It was the complete opposite.

Mr. Johnson was tired of the bank calling him, so he went on to pay for the other vehicle even though it was not in his possession. He trusted Nathan would give him the vehicle on the strength of their past relationship as coworkers. I too, would still ask for the vehicle and for him to return it to John, which to this day he has not. I would also ask for the money he owed so that I could move out of the home, which he ignored. He continuously demanded I stay, and not move out because we have a child on the way.

In the meantime, late notices were getting mailed to the house. The mortgage was three months late. Why would he tell me I could stay knowing this house could go into foreclosure? The second vehicle was still listed on my credit report, and it was still showing me in debt. Therefore, applying for a home had to be postponed until my credit cleared. I needed to come up with a plan quickly. Nathan could not be trusted, and his words were worth nothing to me. He began to text me from fake numbers because he was blocked from my phone. He sent pictures of him and his new girlfriend, the young lady I saw him walk out of the condo with.

Again, it was all so hurtful. Many days I could not breathe. I was fighting the pain so hard. The same girl's purse I found in the truck, I left my number in there for her to call me, and she did. She told me she and Nathan had been dating since February and they were serious. She told me that she had a key to the condo and they went everywhere together. She even named some of the same spots he took me to on dates. She sent text messages of the same conversations Nathan and I used to have. For example, "You are my favorite person. Will you marry me one day?" It was crazy, it was sickening. I now wanted to take his life. It was confirmation I was a part of a narcissistic cycle.

THE MOVE OUT

I called my best friend, Corey. He was one of my friends that Nathan had me cut off early on. I explained to him the whole story and told him I needed his help. Corey has been a very good friend of mine since I was seven years old. We used to play outside together in our younger days. His family had become my family and vice versa. Corey is a truck driver and is always on the road, so he called his brother and cousin to help me get my things out of the home. There was no "I told you so." He was there for me. Corey warned me about Nathan early on and knew I could do better. They came the next day, including my dad. All helping unscrew beds and taking what was mine out of the home. It hurt me so much because my baby loved his room. He did not want to leave the new house, as he would call it.

I fought back tears as they were putting things in the truck, taking pictures down, and loading the furniture. It took everything in me to stay strong. I prayed to God to give me the strength to get through this. He did not answer at that moment, but He was answering and preparing me to become stronger by the day. They continued to load up the truck, pulled off, and headed to the storage unit to drop the items off. Weeks later, I drove by the house and observed his mom and sisters had moved into it. These folks got a whole house off my dime. Another scam they accomplished as a family. The only thing I left behind in that house were my wedding things, I took everything.

This was the most humbling time of my life. I had to go stay with one of my sisters for a few weeks until I was able to get back on my feet. My family knew that I had a lot of pride and that I did not want to have to stay with somebody. I searched for apartments and all, so we could have somewhere to live, but she insisted that I did not and wanted me to save money for the new baby. My daughter was due in August 2021. It made sense and I swallowed my pride and moved in with my sister. I also stayed with a family friend who I called my cousin for about two weeks. Neither asked me for a dime. They wanted me to save money. Here I am again, blessed and highly favored. The Bible reads, "Trust in the Lord with all your heart and lean not on your own understanding (Proverbs 3:5 KJV)." I have always had a relationship with God. This was the first obstacle in my life I had to fight with His Word. It was the only thing I knew how to do. I would call family and friends to vent to, but I would still feel empty after I got off the phone. My heart would still ache badly. Many nights, I wished I would die in my sleep. I took out additional life insurance policies making my son's father, my sister, and my mom beneficiaries. I did the same with my banks.

At this point, I am now six months pregnant with my daughter, Lyric Noelle. I can now feel her kicks and punches. It was like she was telling me to keep fighting. Every time I would sink in pity, she would kick, it was magical. Feeling her kick gave me the extra strength that I needed to keep going with my son. I knew my life was dedicated to my children and that my heartache was not important enough to handicap or take me out. The devil was not going to win, God loved me too much. I was not about to feel sorry for myself anymore. I was worried about being embarrassed by my family and friends. I was so disappointed in myself. When I was younger this was not the life I pictured. I was always the pretty popular girl at school with long hair, light skinned, and an athlete. I was the fun outgoing girl all throughout elementary, middle, and high school. In college, I was focused and was involved in many organizations and sat on executive boards.

However, here I am, single after a week of walking down the aisle. Here I am, with two children out of wedlock with two different fathers. This is something I never thought I would experience. I wanted a husband and a family. I wanted to raise my children in a two-parent household so badly because I did not have that. I knew how negatively it affected me growing up. My mom was awesome, but as a little girl, I still wanted a father in the house. I hated seeing my mom alone and taking care of everything on her own with three children. She made it happen, but I knew she deserved a loving man. She was so great of a person. My sisters and I had everything!

She dedicated her life to us and still does. She has now extended her love to our children. They weren't lying when they said a mother's job is never done.

No More Tears

It is now June 2021; my son and I are living with my oldest sister and her family. I am working with a family friend, who is currently my realtor. I am smoothing out the last few things on my credit report. I look forward to moving into my new construction home before the end of the year. The town house I am looking to purchase is nice but not in a good area. However, it is all I could afford.

My son is healthy and having the time of his life spending the summer with his father. My daughter is healthy and growing well. My mind is at peace, and I know God is holding me throughout my journey. My family and close friends have been supportive of my healing process. I am defeating my pain slowly, but surely. What the devil tried to use to destroy me, I overcame with God's love. I sold my wedding ring to my former supervisor at the police department I used to work for. We are still good friends. He is giving it to his wife for their anniversary. The ring is still beautiful. She will love it!

I shed no more tears. I can think of Nathan and the situation without crying and wishing things had never played out this way. I am stronger and fiercer than ever. I gained new love for myself; it was long overdue. This was the most time I ever spent with myself. I mean every second, minute, and hour of the day I would look for ways to pour into myself. I would read God's Word; it is my biggest sword.

I knew I had to mentally snap out of it because I must have a healthy mind to bring my daughter into this world and continue raising her and her brother in the best way. I owe that to them both. I turned my pain into prosperity and purpose. I am currently the owner of a logistics company, Together We Will Prosper Logistics, LLC and I look forward to making millions. God kept me; He is still keeping me. I am grateful for my new journey. After the pain, I was able to write my story, my first book of the past year of my life and still writing and documenting my journey. I pray it helps the next young lady who falls in love with a narcissist, I pray my daughter never comes across one. I pray I guide her and my son to the Word of God and know that they will always have God and myself to lean on.

Prayer for Protection

Dear God,

Lord, I am facing challenges that I cannot overcome on my own, and I feel afraid and uncertain. Please fight my battles for me and protect me from harm. Give me the courage and strength to stand firm in the face of adversity and to trust in Your unfailing love.

Thank you for Your love and grace, and for always being there for me. I trust in Your power, and I know that you will fight for me and give me the victory.

In Jesus' name, Amen.

Chapter 7

Regaining My Power

CHAPTER 7

REGAINING MY POWER

It is now December 2021. Everything was aligning for me, and life felt normal again. The pain is slowly, but surely going away. I was focusing on God, my children, my family, and my bag. I am cutting people out of my life who are not aligned. My beautiful daughter is now four months old. She is healthy and absolutely perfect. She is the most beautiful little girl in the world, my gift from God. My business has grown and I have secured several relationships in the trucking industry. I never thought I would take an interest in the trucking industry. Law enforcement was always my thing.

During this time, I am preparing to move out of my sister's house. I am experiencing miracles after miracles, which is how I was able to buy my house. A friend of mine sold me her house for $30,000 below the asking price. She had no idea of what was going on with me. She just called to catch up and see how I was doing. During the conversation, we both discovered she was selling her home and I was looking to purchase a home.

She offered to sell her house to me and mentioned she would even go down $30,000 on the asking price. I could not believe it. I was in the process of closing on another property and canceled it quickly to purchase her house. We closed in 30 days. God was truly moving in my life because that was a miracle. I was so happy because I told my sister to give me six months and it was around month seven when I made the move. My sister and her husband were a great support system during the time when I needed them.

I felt proud that I was walking in my calling and had found my purpose. Bringing 2021 to a close was a refreshing experience for me. I felt a chapter was closed, old baggage was left, and I refused to take any excuses into the next year. I picked my head up and went to work holding God's hand and keeping Him close.

I am extremely thankful for how far God has brought me, and everything that took place was supposed to happen the way it did. I no longer have regrets or negative thoughts. I am no longer depressed, embarrassed, or suicidal. I have accepted that God is the author of my life and I will trust Him in whatever life may bring. I know to not ignore your gut feelings; it is there to protect you.

Also working hard on your craft is very important in life. We only get one so never spend it being sad over spoiled milk. Life will teach you different lessons that may be hurtful to accept. It is how you take on the challenge and what you do with it that will give you the inner strength you need to keep pushing in life to reach your highest being. I have accepted that my way is not the best way, but God's way is. I am enjoying living in my purpose and sharing my testimony. I enjoy helping many women who are fighting silent battles and spreading awareness to Domestic and Narcissistic Abuse.

"Not everyone who gets into an abusive relationship is insecure, timid, and lacks self-esteem. Some are strong, confident, successful people who were manipulated into relationships with devious people. People who took advantage of their goodness and beat them down so bad they forgot to love themselves."-

Maria Consiglio.

"Never be ashamed of your story. It will inspire others."
- Adam Bandelli

JANUARY 2023

In one year, God has worked tremendously in my life. It was Him; He gets all the credit. I am amazed to see His grace, mercy, and promise work in my life. This transition has been the most self-rewarding process to witness. I feel so different and whole. My walk is even different, my confidence, my self-worth everything has God written all over it. I am watching God move right before my eyes and it is amazing to witness.

My business is prospering. I made no mistake with the name, Together We Will Prosper Logistics Dispatching firm. My firm is now a six-figure dispatching company within a year. I am taking each day to gain knowledge on what is best for my clients while they tackle the roads. I have been interviewed on the Truck N Hustle Podcast as a new dispatching company who is growing in business. Mastering every level of running a dispatching firm along with starting my security company, Abundance

International Protective Services. My stepfather is coaching me along the way because he also owns a security company. He assures my T's are crossed and I's are dotted. Yes, my mom found her true love after raising her children, true soulmates. We connect mostly on our passion for creating our own empires. Our conversations are educational, and he is excited for me to start a new business.

I have learned that God's love is the greatest love you can ever experience. I no longer lack self-worth, settle for less, or ignore red flags. It feels so amazing to finally live in my purpose, trust God's plan, and feel Him directing my steps. I have had the honor to tell my story in rooms I never thought I would be in. Also, in 2022 I was a nominee in the Motivation Maven category at the Galentine's Day Gala and now I am nominated in 2023 for, "Woman of Logistics," and landed the win at the ceremony this year in February. It is a beautiful all red event hosted for women in business. I have secured numerous contracts with carriers, brokers, and shippers. I have made relationships in the industry that I cherish. Also, I have better and genuine friendships, business partners, and spend more quality time with my family. Never isolate yourself from your family. No matter how bad your family can get on your nerves, their love is unconditional and forgiving. My family still loves me and has my back. They admire my growth. They love my children and I for who we are. My family truly helped me through my healing process.

The first step to healing was taking accountability. I could blame Nathan all day for everything, but I had to take accountability for my choices in that situation. Once I took accountability and accepted the role I played in the relationship, I had more clarity about the situation. The second step was to forgive myself. We all go through challenging times and don't always make the best decisions. However, we have to give ourselves grace and learn from our mistakes. Although some days may be triggering, I give myself grace and allow God to lead me. The third step to healing is making a decision to improve your life. As you decide to improve internally, your actions will reflect that improvement in the decisions you make. When you know better, you will do better, and with that you will use better judgment. I decided to truly believe He wants the best for me and when the time is right, I will know my person was specifically sent by God. The fourth step is to never allow anyone or anything to negatively impact your mental health. I vowed to never ignore red flags. I promise to never lose myself again or jeopardize my mental health for anybody no matter the relationship. The fifth step is to keep moving forward every day no matter what challenges you may face. I made a promise to myself to move on and along when things do not align or feel right in my heart.

My final thoughts to all women who are experiencing toxic relationships, trust God, and do not ignore your intuition, it is there to protect you. Always know God loves you so much. He will never send you someone who will hurt you. He is not a God of pain, confusion, or abuse. He is a God of love, peace, and prosperity. . Everything is aligning and is on God's timing and plan. My advice to you is to trust God, wipe your tears, up your hustle, and prosper. I am just getting started and I will meet you at the top, where there are no limits to God's promise. My message to you is to move on even when it hurts.

Prayer for Restoration

Dear God,

I come to You for restoration and healing. I know that You are a God of restoration and renewal, and that You can bring new life and hope to my situation. Lord, I pray for restoration in my family, my health, my finances, and every other area of my life where I need your healing touch. I ask that You bring wholeness and healing to the broken places in my life.

Please help me to let go of any bitterness or resentment that may be hindering my restoration. Give me the strength to forgive and move forward in faith. I trust in Your healing power, and I believe You will restore what has been lost or damaged in my life.

In Jesus' name, Amen.

LETTER TO MY HEAVENLY FATHER

Dear Lord,

Thank you Lord for saving me from destruction. Thank you for hearing my prayers and stepping in. Thank you for blessing me more than I can imagine and helping me define my purpose. I am a better mom, person, and friend. I have scaled my business with your help. I had no idea I could create an empire and be great at it. Thank you for giving me the vision to create multiple businesses. Thank you for allowing me to dream and protecting my children and I.

Lord, thank you for the family who still loves and shows up for me. Thank you for allowing me to lean on them no matter what. We have been through a lot, and my family still and will always love me. Thank you for giving me the strength to leave and lean on true love. I trust You during this transition. Although this is hard, I trust You.

Thank you for this new journey and for blessing my children and I. I trust You as You continue to order my steps. It's us three now, and I need your help. I pray we lack nothing and grow deeper in Your Word. I am ready to live out your purpose for my life. I no longer want to do it my way, and I am tired.

Lastly, thank You for always staying faithful and keeping Your promise. I love You; I honor You, and I am beyond grateful. I cannot even fathom what more You are about to do in my life and with people tied to me. I am ready to live out Your plan for me.

Love,
Your Daughter

LETTER TO MY DAUGHTER LYRIC NOELLE

Dear Lyric,

I love you so much little girl. It has been a journey since the day I conceived you. I remember riding in the car to my doctor's appointment and I began to bleed like a waterfall. I screamed and cried. I then pulled over to the side of the roadway. I knew I had lost you; there were blood puddles in the driver's seat. Your dad had taken me to the doctor earlier that day due to spotting, but it stopped. I was only about two red lights from the doctor's office. I got back into my vehicle and continued to drive. Once I arrived, I ran into the doctor's office and all the nurses rushed to me. They immediately called for an ambulance seeing that my pants were filled with blood. The ladies in the waiting room were already sending their condolences. It was not a pretty sight to witness.

I get to the hospital, and I am rushed into the first room available. Doctors rush in and call out codes. One doctor undressed me waist down, looks and confirms it was a miscarriage. My heart is broken. I lay there praying while they cleaned me up. They told me to wait for the ultrasound tech to look, so they could see what was going on. The ultrasound tech came into the room and rolled me into another room. She then pulled up my shirt and began to do her job with finding the last of you on the ultrasound. I saw the look on her face, she was shocked! There was a strong heartbeat, and you were still inside me wiggling around. The tech stated, *"This is a miracle. I have to take you back to your room and the doctor will have to go over this with you."* I began to thank GOD; He was my doctor. You were still with me, fighting. I was already so proud of you.

Since that day, I knew you were my little fighter. I knew you were tough. I knew you already had the gift to prove any doctor or anyone wrong. I left the hospital that night and the doctor diagnosed me with *Threatening Miscarriage,* which means they were counting on seeing me back in the next few weeks to treat me for a miscarriage. I threw the paperwork away. I knew we had already won that battle and you were here to stay.

Lyric, I am sorry your dad and I did not work out. I tried hard to raise you in a two-parent household. Although it did not work out with your father and I, I know it is still God's plan. God has already prepared the way; He is now preparing us. I promise you will not miss a beat.

I cannot promise life will not be challenging. However, I promise to listen to you, not judge you, wipe your tears, guide you, and teach you the Word of God. I promise to always be here for you and never leave your side. We may not see eye to eye as you get older, but I promise to always end on the same page. You cannot have a boyfriend until you are 40 (haha) but when you get to the dating stage, come to me, talk to me, and do not be afraid of any reactions. I will only tell you what is best for you. I will still love you, no matter your darkest secrets. Do not hide anything from me. I am the closest one to you on this earth to protect you. We will get through anything together; we will see it through as a family.

Love,
Your Mommy

Letter To My Son Grayson

Dear Grayson,

You are my best friend, my first born. You are the son I always wanted. You are such a gentleman and so funny. Thank you for loving me and always reminding me that I am the best and how pretty I am. Thank you for always telling me how you feel when you think I am doing too much.

Lol. I pray God continues to protect you and order your steps to be the best you can be. The love you show your sister is so amazing to witness. You will stand up for her against anybody and I love it. Thank you for helping with the trucks and being so interested in mommy's business. You are literally my biggest supporter.

Son, as you grow older, keep God first. Protect yourself and always treat women with love and respect. Never say or do things that will break a person's soul. Always follow God, so when you have your family one day you will lead them correctly. When you are faced with life obstacles, open your Bible, write and pray for strength as you grow from a boy to a man. There will be times you want to give up. Remember your mom will always have your back. I will always be here for you. Share everything with me. We will tackle life together. It is so amazing to watch you grow up. You are already an all-star athlete like I used to be. I can't wait to travel the world with you and watch you be great. Thank you for understanding why I am hard on you. You are such a person of grace, love, and mercy.

Your dad is your best friend. Keep that relationship. There may be things you can share with him rather than with me and that is ok. Always know that you have us both to love and lean on throughout life. You have witnessed first-hand how hard I work and at five years old, you motivate me to keep going. It is so crazy, but your understanding of life already is unremarkable. I love seeing you state your affirmations every morning. I love that you are so confident. Everything you see me working towards, know that I will pass the torch to you one day, when I am old and gray. Grayson, keep Prosper Logistics close to you and your family for generational wealth. Teach your family to lead, follow their dreams, take risks and to lean on God. I love you son so much; I know you are going to grow into a great man. You are my baby boy, and it is my duty to make sure you enjoy your youth years and teach you the ropes of life. Buckle up, we have a world to change.

Love,
Your mommy

Proverbs 22:6

"Train up a child in the way he should go; even when he is old he will not depart from it."

Letter To My Mother

Dear Mom,

As I sit down to write this letter, I am filled with so much gratitude and love for you. I want to take this opportunity to thank you for everything you have done for me and for being the amazing mother you are.

Growing up, I always felt safe and loved in your presence. You always comforted me when I was sad, celebrated with me when I was happy, and guided me when I needed direction. Your unwavering support and love have been a constant source of strength for me, and I cannot thank you enough.

As I have grown older, I have realized how much you have sacrificed for our family. You have always put our needs before yours, and your selflessness is truly inspiring. You have shown me what it means to be a strong, loving, and caring woman, and I am so grateful for that.

I also want to thank you for the countless times you have encouraged me to pursue my dreams and never give up. Your belief in me has given me the courage to pursue my passions and to never settle for less than I deserve.

I want you to know that I love you more than words can express. I will always be grateful for everything you have done for me. Thank you for being my rock, confidante, and best friend. I am so blessed to have you as my mother. Your teachings and raising me in the church, allowed me to reflect on God's word to overcome a situation that almost broke me. As a mom, I would never want my kids to face what I faced, so I understand how you may be feeling. However, I am stronger and wiser. Again, thank you for loving me and always doing the best you could, while raising me. It took courage to write this book, to help many women suffering silently. With your love, I stand tall and will now live on purpose.

With all my love and gratitude,
Your daughter Kyra

SCRIPTURES TO BREAK GENERATIONAL CURSES

Deuteronomy 28:8

The Lord will send a blessing on your barns and on everything you put your hand to. The Lord your God will bless you in the land he is giving you.

Jeremiah 30:17

I will restore you to health and heal your wounds, declares the Lord.

John 8:32

You will know the truth, and the truth will set you free.

Genesis 28:15

Behold, I am with you and will keep you wherever you go and will bring you back to this land. For I will not leave you until I have done what I have promised you.

Proverbs 16:4

The Lord has made everything for its own purpose, even the wicked or the day of trouble.

Isaiah 46:4

I am he; I am he who will sustain you. I have made you and I will carry you. I will sustain you and I will rescue you.

Psalms 119:24

Your testimonies also are my delight and my counselors.

Psalm 32:8

I will instruct you and teach you in the way you should go; I will guide you with my eye.

III John 1:2

Beloved, I pray that you may prosper in all things and be in health, just as your soul prospers.

About The Author

Kyra King is an entrepreneur in the trucking industry and is now an inspirational speaker and booked for speaking engagements. She built her business from the ground up in May of 2021, due to major life changes. Kyra has always been actively involved in her community. She created a basketball camp for small kids and formed a mentoring group for minority males. This camp took place during the summer in her community at a local church. In the same community, Kyra served as a former police officer, detective, and worked in security in the private sector.

You can connect with Ms. King on social media:

Instagram @_prosper_logistics

Youtube: @TruckingAlongWithKy

Facebook: Prosper Logistics

Made in the USA
Columbia, SC
09 October 2023

23902141R00065